GRANT WRITING FOR IMPACT WORKBOOK

A Practical Resource for Developing School Grants

Peggy Downs

D1568147

Granting Your Vision
School Grants Services by Peggy Downs

TABLE OF CONTENTS

Introduction

DEVELOP A PLAN TO MEET YOUR SCHOOL GOALS

Grants can help schools provide support and opportunities for their students and have greater impact on their communities. I work with school leaders, founders, and teachers to find, develop, and manage grants. To do this, you need resources developed specifically for you.

Through my business and blog, "Granting Your Vision," I provide training, support, and grant-writing services to help you reach your goals. With twenty years' experience in charter schools, I can answer your questions about grants.

What you do is important. Grants can help you do more. My experience in leadership and grant writing helps me understand what you need.

Let's work together to help you do more. You can do this! I can help.

Bonus Offer: Grant-Writing Action Plan ~ 20% Discount

As a reader of this book, you have a special offer waiting for you. I am offering the **Grant Writing Action Plan** at 20 percent off the current price. With my help, you can develop a plan to meet your school goals.

This bonus offer includes a two-hour consultation, a written action plan developed based on your input, and a follow-up call after the plan has been implemented. We'll take my five-step strategy from *Grant Writing for Impact* and apply them to your specific situation, with coaching and resources from me personally.

This offer is limited to availability. Contact me soon to schedule your first call.

Visit www.peggydowns.com/workwithme for more information or contact me for current pricing on this special bonus offer. peggydowns@gmail.com

Granting Your Vision
School Grants Services by Peggy Downs

HOW TO USE THIS WORKBOOK

Grant Writing for Impact Workbook – A Practical Resource for Developing School Grants is designed to be a companion resource for *Grant Writing for Impact*. In case you have purchased this workbook separately, I've included the strategies and main points from the original book. Many of the pages in this book might not make sense without the original book, so I recommend that they be purchased together.

Adding grants to your leadership toolkit can help you fulfill your school's vision and meet your goals. Review this diagram to understand the complete system for developing your school grants program.

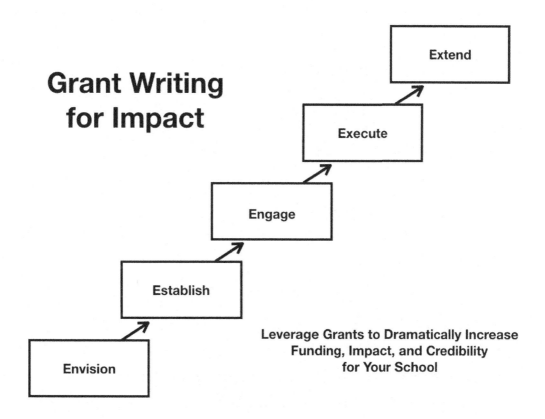

I.   **Envision** the program you want to develop

Focus: Develop your vision and goals, aligned with your school's mission

•   Articulate your vision

- Align your goals
- Amplify your impact

2. **Establish** systems and teams to support your grants program

Focus: Make sure your school is grant-ready

- Gather documents and information
- Establish your grants committee
- Make your school grant-ready

3. **Engage** partners who share your vision

Focus: Create partnerships with grantmakers who want to help you meet your goals

- Understand various types of grants
- Understand what grantmakers need from you
- Find grants that meet your goals

4. **Execute** your plan to meet your goals

Focus: Put it all together to prepare your proposal

- Start with the basics
- Identify the problem you will solve
- Develop a detailed action plan

5. **Extend** your vision with long-term planning

Focus: Create reliable funding and strong partnerships to sustain your vision

- Build a pipeline
- Improve capacity to lead and manage grants
- Beyond grants—build your school support pyramid

I've developed this workbook with the school leader in mind. I am assuming you have access to the school information you need to write grants and that you are a decision maker within your organization. You may be an administrator, board member, new school founder, or in some other leadership role. I hope these pages help you develop a clearer understanding of your school's mission and how grants and other fundraising activities can help you achieve your goals.

INTRODUCTION

I have reproduced brief excerpts from the main book, *Grant Writing for Impact*, to help you understand the activities in this workbook. Please refer to the main book for more information. All workbook pages are found in the order you might need them as you read the main book. Feel free to skip any pages that do not apply to your situation.

It's time to start developing a successful grants program for your school. Let's get started.

Peggy Downs

Envision

Envision the Program
You Want to Develop

WHAT TRANSFORMATION WILL YOU PROMISE?

As a school leader, you send a message about your school in every communication. A clear message about your school's potential to transform lives can improve your success with enrollment, staff recruitment, and grant applications.

Let's borrow some ideas from the experts in marketing and look at your message with fresh eyes.

Features

A school's features are the basic details such as:

- Mission and vision statement
- Grades served
- Curriculum and instructional philosophy
- Activities and special programs offered
- Location and facility

List your school's basic features here:

_____

_____

_____

_____

_____

_____

Benefits

To talk about benefits, you must see your school from the perspective of the student or family. What are the benefits that your school offers to students? List them below.

_____

_____

_____

_____

_____

_____

Results

Results are not about how many students participated in a program. Results will celebrate what happened BECAUSE they participated. Results show that you are keeping your promises. List the results of your key programs below.

_____

_____

_____

_____

_____

_____

Transformation

Now for the real question: How are you transforming the lives of your students? If your vision statement is effective, it gives you the roadmap. It tells you what transformation is expected when you fulfill your mission.

Review your vision statement and extract the key promises your school has made. Rewrite that idea into an affirmative statement that will resonate with your stakeholders.

_____

_____

_____

_____

_____

_____

_____

_____

FOCUS ON THE MISSION

Leading the mission means that everyone at your charter school deeply understands and embraces the mission of the school. Follow these steps to complete an audit of your school's implementation of your mission statement.

1. What is your mission statement? Write it in the space below.

_____

_____

_____

_____

_____

_____

_____

_____

2. Review your mission statement, and break it down into key elements. Highlight or underline each element.

For example, if your mission statement is like this one, you would have seven key elements to measure:

> Our mission is to create an <u>academically rigorous</u> (1), <u>progressive learning environment</u> (2) that <u>engages each student's unique strengths</u> (3) and <u>intellect</u> (4), <u>fosters creativity</u> (5) and <u>critical thinking skills</u> (6), and <u>cultivates global citizenship</u> (7).

3. Look at each key element and determine how it is impacted by your:

- Board training and meeting practices
- Curriculum (textbooks, online resources, standards-alignment, content, and skills mastery)
- Communications (schoolwide, classroom, website, print, etc.)
- Community outreach
- Facilities
- Fundraising and donations
- Hiring practices and employment policies
- Instructional methods, including assessment, homework, and grading
- Professional development, including onboarding of new hires
- Policies such as dress code, discipline, and volunteering
- Security
- Technology resources

Notes

_____

_____

_____

_____

_____

_____

_____

_____

4. Using what you have learned, write a paragraph or two that answers these questions.

- What will students be able to do as a result of your school's program, and how is this different from other schools?

- What is our definition of success?

- How will we know we achieved it?

_____

_____

_____

_____

_____

_____

_____

_____

_____

_____

_____

_____

_____

_____

5. Now, decide how you will strengthen your alignment to the mission and make a plan. Sort the areas you find that need to be updated into several "buckets," such as:

- Policies (need board approval)
- Budget items (need money and approval)
- Training and communications (need time to make changes)

6. Determine timelines and priorities for the changes you identify.

7. Communicate your findings with key personnel and board members.

8. Hold yourself accountable for meeting your goals.

Example

This mission statement is from a school I once led. I've underlined the key elements.

> The purpose of the Academy is to provide <u>excellence</u> and <u>fairness</u> in education through a <u>common educational foundation</u>. Our goal is to provide each student with <u>knowledge</u>, <u>skills</u>, and <u>character</u> through strong <u>parent-teacher-student partnerships</u>.

As I implemented this mission, I zeroed in on the words "excellence," demonstrated through knowledge and skills, and "fairness," demonstrated through character. This led to our tag line, "Building Knowledge and Character." We identified a national curriculum that established a common educational foundation. We also worked to define and develop parent-teacher-student partnerships.

From that point on, it became a simple process of filtering all decisions through those key elements. If a proposal did not serve to build knowledge or character in our students, or to support parent-teacher-student partnerships, it was not a match. We used that standard in all decision-making.

- **Looking to create an annual festival?** Make sure it connects to our curriculum and engages students in enhanced learning opportunities.

- **Wondering how to structure our parent-teacher conferences?** Consider the parent-teacher-student partnership and ensure that all members have a voice in school conferences.

- **Reviewing the school's discipline policy?** Ensure that it is fair and that students have an opportunity to learn from their mistakes.
- **Planning a fundraising activity?** Find an activity that will help students to gain new skills or build character.

Clarity and consistency can strengthen your message for grants proposals, marketing, and recruiting as it improves your overall school program.

How Will You Improve Your Focus on the Mission?

_____

_____

_____

_____

_____

_____

_____

_____

_____

_____

_____

_____

_____

DEVELOP YOUR GUIDING STATEMENT

What is your personal vision for your school? Can you turn the abstract language of your mission statement into a personal agenda that drives the school toward achieving the goals that were set in your founding documents?

Now, take that set of personal goals and use it to develop programs and projects, supported by grants, which move your students closer to that vision.

Example

Using the mission statement for my charter school shown above, I created this guiding statement:

> *I will be a leader who finds the balance between excellence and fairness in all my decisions, building stronger partnerships and implementing our approved curriculum based on current assessment data and best practices.*

What Is Your Guiding Statement?

_____

_____

_____

_____

_____

_____

_____

_____

DEVELOP YOUR PROGRAM IDEA

A purpose statement expresses the basic idea of your grant proposal. Use the questions below to develop your idea so that you can begin searching for grant partners and developing your grant proposal.

Make a List

Make a list of all the things that come to mind. Don't judge or hold back on any of them. Walk around the school and take notes. Talk to your staff to see what they think. What problems are you dealing with? What do you need in order to provide better support for your students? Write your thoughts and ideas here.

_____

_____

_____

_____

_____

_____

_____

_____

Write Your Purpose Statement

Grants have lots of ways of asking questions, but they nearly all boil down to these same four elements. These elements form the basis of your purpose statement.

- **People** – Who needs your help? Be specific. Identify a subgroup of students who need your help. You most likely want to help someone _catch up_ or _get ahead_.

ENVISION

- **Problem** – What problem are you trying to solve? This problem should be aligned with your school's mission and grant goals.

- **Plan** – By doing what? What you want to do that requires money from the grant?

- **Progress** – What will be better? What do you expect to happen and how will you know if you were successful?

Who needs your help?

People:

_____

_____

_____

_____

_____

What problem do you want to solve?

Problem:

_____

_____

_____

_____

_____

What do you want to do?

Plan:

_____

_____

_____

_____

_____

_____

What are your expected outcomes and how will you know if you met your goals?

Progress:

_____

_____

_____

_____

_____

_____

Write a purpose statement for the grant proposal:

_____ (who) struggle with

_____ (problem). I want to help by

_____ (doing what) so that

_____ (what will be better?).

For example: Many high school students struggle with organization and time management. I want to help by providing a specialized curriculum to teach these skills in Advisory so that they can be successful in school and in their future careers.

Write your final purpose statement here:

_____

_____

_____

_____

_____

_____

_____

_____

_____

TIPS FOR SUCCESS

Follow these tips as you begin to build your school grants program.

1. **Get your school grant-ready.** Review your financial policies and leadership skills to determine the size and type of grants you can manage.

2. **Find the right grant.** Use a targeted approach to search for and apply to the right grants. Be patient and wait for the best match.

3. **Read the guidelines.** Be absolutely sure that a particular foundation or government grant is appropriate for your school. Is your school eligible? Has the source funded charter schools before? Does the organization want to fund programs like yours? Does it work with agencies in your community?

4. **Get organized...now.** At slow times in your schedule, gather the documents you are likely to need. Save a copy of your recent annual audit in your grants file. Make a copy of your 501(c)(3) letter, business license, and organization chart for your files.

5. **Use the grantmaker's language.** In order to make it clear that you are concerned about the granting organization's goals, use language that reflects their values and priorities.

6. **Repeat yourself when you have to.** A certain amount of repetition is unavoidable. Different sections will ask for information in different ways, and you will need to summarize the information in the abstract or executive summary. Choose key points that deserve repetition.

7. **Keep it easy to read.** Break up your text with shorter paragraphs, charts and tables, and subheadings.

8. **Follow the outline.** Use the application's headings in your document, and keep them in order. The grant application is designed for the funder's convenience, not yours. Keep your documents and responses in the same order they are given to you.

9. **Review the rubric.** Refer to the grant rubric or description of how the grant will be scored. Watch for any weighted categories or special priorities that may not show up in the application itself.

REFLECTIONS

Reflect on what we've discussed and complete the following statements before moving on to the next chapter.

1. I learned:

_____

_____

_____

_____

_____

_____

2. I loved:

_____

_____

_____

_____

_____

_____

3. I wonder:

_____

_____

_____

_____

_____

_____

_____

4. I plan to:

_____

_____

_____

_____

_____

_____

_____

_____

Establish

Establish Systems and Teams to Support Your Grants Program

QUICK-START CHECKLIST

This checklist combines all the activities you might need to complete to develop your grants program. Check off each activity as you complete it, and make a note of what tasks you still need to do or need to learn.

Get Ready for Grants

✔ *Check each box when you have completed the task.*

☐ Plan time to write a strong grant proposal.

☐ Establish a grants committee or support team.

☐ Assign staff to run the program and manage grant-reporting requirements.

☐ Create or update policies and procedures to support grant program requirements.

☐ Save a copy of your IRS Nonprofit letter with your grants documents.

Develop Your Program Idea

☐ Brainstorm ideas to start or expand a project or program at your school.

☐ Decide who will benefit most from this project or plan.

☐ Estimate how much this project or program will cost.

☐ Decide when you need the money.

☐ Develop an action plan for your idea.

Choose Your Grant

☐ Download the free report: School Grants You Can Use.

☐ Create a free account at GetEdFunding.com.

☐   Search for grants that meet your needs.

☐   Review each potential grant to ensure it's a good match:
[ ] Purpose   [ ] Deadline   [ ] Funding Amount   [ ] Eligibility

☐   Choose one grant and review the application carefully.

☐   Gather all documents required for the application.

Write Your Grant Proposal

☐   Download any templates provided in the application.

☐   Review the application questions carefully and plan your responses.

☐   Write your responses to each question in a separate document.

☐   Ensure you meet all guidelines for page count, word count, and templates.

☐   Review and edit; use spell check.

☐   Copy your answers into the grant application.

☐   Attach all required documents.

☐   Submit your grant application.

☐   Take note of the process and date for notification of awards; make a note in your calendar.

Implement Your Grant Project

☐   Review grant notification:

- If you are not approved, try again at another time or with another grant opportunity; send a thank you note and request feedback on your proposal.

- If you are approved, review the proposal and be sure you understand the terms and conditions.

☐ Review and sign the grant agreement.

☐ Implement the program or project in accordance with the grant proposal; do what you said you would do.

☐ Track all expenditures and prepare reports as required in the agreement.

Close Out Your Grant

☐ Submit reports and expense receipts to meet all deadlines.

☐ Share your success with the school community.

☐ Thank the grantmaker; send photos of the project if appropriate.

☐ Plan for your next grant proposal.

DOCUMENTS AND INFORMATION

This checklist will help you gather most of the information that will be needed for grant applications, but not all of these documents may be required for your application. Check the grant application and RFP/RFG for specific information on what is required for this grant.

Basic Documents and Information

Basic documents include general information for your school. Save these to use again for future grants and other purposes.

Gather Basic Documents

✔ *Check each box when you have completed the task.*

☐ 501(c) (3) Letter

☐ School mission and vision, brief history

☐ Key staff members (list of names, titles)

☐ Board members (list of names, officers)

☐ Other grants you have received (list, brief summary with donor's name and purpose of grant)

Additional Basic Documents and Information

These may not be needed for the smaller grants or very straightforward applications. Check the rubric and application for to see what you will need. Save these to use again for future grants and other purposes.

Gather Additional Documents

☐ EIN (Employer Identification Number)

☐ DUNS (Dunn & Bradstreet Number)

☐ Letters of support

- [ ] Organizational chart

- [ ] Marketing materials

- [ ] Recent publicity, honors, and achievements

- [ ] Audited budget (.pdf for online applications)

- [ ] Current P&L or recent budget summary (the monthly budget reviewed by the board of directors)

Information for Specific Grants

The following information will be specific to this grant, and probably will need to be created or edited to meet the goals of this proposal. Save these to use for reference, as you may be able to recycle much of this work for future grants.

Additional Information You May Need

- [ ] Description of why your school is eligible for this grant.

- [ ] Description of how the project aligns with your school's mission and vision, school goals and strategic plan, and how it is related to the donor's goals and values.

- [ ] Details on key staff and board members – Describe any special skills, experience, and credentials that make your team especially qualified for this project. Include major contributions from board members or specialized expertise that may apply to the grant proposal.

- [ ] Description of any partners you are collaborating with and their role in the project – Grant funders are often looking for programs that improve collaboration between entities, especially between schools and other nonprofits.

- [ ] SMART goals/objectives describe what you will do, how you will measure your actions, and what change you expect to see when the program is completed.

☐ Budget – Word table or Excel spreadsheet with overall total amount requested, amount per category if needed, line items with dollar amounts and vendor names, and a brief description of each item.

☐ Timeline – Word table or Excel spreadsheet; map out the basic milestones and tasks that must be done to accomplish this project. On some grants, you will need to assign a responsible party to each task.

☐ Narrative – Connect budget, timeline, and project goals. Describe your project in strong, confident language.

- What is the problem you want to solve?
- What do you want to do about it?
- How will you do it?
- When will you do it?
- How do the expenses support what you will do?
- What will be different when you are done?

☐ Evaluation includes clear outcomes and measurements.

☐ Plan for sustainability is viable and realistic.

Notes

_____

_____

_____

_____

_____

_____

_____

DEVELOP A COMMITTEE CHARGE STATEMENT

Write a charge statement for your grants committee and use it to guide your decisions. A charge statement defines the committee's purpose, authority, structure, and responsibilities. A charge statement has five elements:

- Mission statement or statement of purpose
- Committee membership
- Authority
- Responsibility
- Meetings

Mission Statement

First, the charge statement gives the mission, the reason the committee exists. Is your committee focused on a particular project or a specific grant? Are you exploring a variety of smaller grants to supplement revenue? Are you hoping to develop a proposal for a major or federal grant?

Write one or two sentences that describe your purpose for this committee.

_____

_____

_____

_____

_____

_____

_____

Membership

Who will participate in this committee, and who decides? Is a board member or the executive director going to chair the committee? Do you have a minimum or maximum number of members in mind? Will you invite staff members or parents? What about community members? Will you work with a grant writer?

Define the committee membership in one or two sentences, including how the chair is appointed and any other requirements.

Authority

Define the committee's authority, describing the process for approving grant programs and setting any limits to this authority. Is your committee limited to focusing on federal grants to support a school expansion? Are you hoping to find a variety of grants to support expanding your tech lab? Are you exploring grants and open to any that support your school improvement goals? Does the committee decide which grants to pursue or do they need approval from someone with greater authority?

Describe your expectations for grant selection and prioritizing, and define who has decision-making authority.

_____

_____

_____

_____

_____

_____

_____

_____

Responsibility

This statement will list the committee's responsibilities, including finding grant opportunities, developing proposals, reporting results to the board of directors, and making progress toward grant-funding goals.

Describe the committee responsibilities in one to two sentences.

_____

_____

_____

_____

_____

_____

_____

_____

Meetings

Depending on your goals, you may need to work furiously for a short time on a pending grant, or you may need to meet less frequently throughout the school year as you become familiar with grant opportunities. Decide who calls the meetings and establish some frame of reference to describe how often the committee will meet.

Define the schedule of meetings and define who is in charge of scheduling meetings.

_____

_____

_____

_____

_____

_____

_____

_____

_____

_____

_____

_____

_____

Example

Here is an example of a grants committee charge statement:

> The Grants Committee works throughout the year to identify and apply for grants. In addition to the Executive Director, the Grants Committee shall consist of at least one teacher and one parent volunteer. The committee is chaired by the Executive Director, who is authorized to establish priorities and determine grant projects that align with school improvement goals and the strategic plan. Any grant proposals over $10,000 must be approved by the Board of Directors prior to submission. The Grants Committee is responsible for identifying appropriate grant opportunities, developing grant proposals, and supporting active grant programs. The Executive Director shall report grant activities to the Board of Directors at least quarterly. The Executive Director is authorized to determine the meeting schedule, based on grant opportunities and priorities.

Create Your Grants Committee Charge Statement

It is best practice to present this statement to the board of directors for discussion and approval. Write your complete charge statement here.

_____

_____

_____

_____

_____

_____

_____

SET THE AGENDA

Your grants committee has an incredibly important job. It is the committee's responsibility to ensure strategic grant-writing efforts for your school. Use your time wisely by setting a strong agenda for each meeting. Consider the following three elements as the foundation for each agenda, and then customize to your needs.

- Establish and review fundraising goals in accordance with the charge statement.

- Set expectations for ongoing research for future grant opportunities. Develop a mix of funding sources through various grants.

- Develop and adjust your action plan, including areas of responsibility, timelines, and evaluation measures.

Use the chart below to plan the agenda for your first grants committee meeting.

Time	Topic	Notes
	Fundraising Goals • Goal Amount • Funding Priorities	
	Expectations • How many grants? • What type of grants? • How will you decide which grants to pursue?	
	Action Plan • What are your next steps to move closer to your goals? • How will you measure progress?	

GRANTS COMMITTEE TASK LIST

You can use this task list to help organize your grants committee. This task list is simply a starting point. Your committee may choose to organize the work in any way that suits you.

Suggested Committee Roles

- **Researcher** – searches for grants, identifies grant opportunities, shares deadlines and documentation requirements with committee

- **Bookkeeper or records keeper** – manages the paperwork (real or digital), grants calendar, and committee task lists

- **Writer** – does most of the actual writing of the proposal and related supporting documents

- **Copyeditor** – edits the draft proposals for accuracy, clarity, and consistency

- **Proposal Coordinator** – leads meetings, reports activity to board of directors or other authority and seeks approval as needed, manages committee in accordance with mission, goals, and agreed tasks. Decides who will be responsible to gather and upload all documents and enter all information into online application and hit "submit."

Committee Tasks

Member	Task
Researcher	Search for grants for priority program goals.
Researcher	Bring recommendations to committee.
Researcher	Plan grant-writing schedule to meet deadline and coordinate with committee.
Researcher	Share RFP and application with committee, highlighting key requirements and necessary documentation.

Member	Task
Records Keeper	Add grant deadline to committee calendar.
Records Keeper	Collect required documents for grant application.
Records Keeper	Contact others as needed to gather related documents and information, such as copy of 501(c)(3) letter and latest audit.
Records Keeper	Track documents and information as received and ensure all requirements are met.
Records Keeper	Take minutes of committee meetings and ensure that all members are meeting commitments for tasks assigned. If not, communicate with Proposal Coordinator for follow-up.
Records Keeper	Keep digital and hard copies of all documents related to committee and grant application.
Writer	Set up account for grant application if needed. Share login and password with Proposal Coordinator, or provide information so Coordinator can set up own account.
Writer	Take notes during committee meetings to develop draft of proposal.
Writer	Bring draft to committee for review and discussion. Continue to refine based on feedback.
Writer	Work with others to create additional documents such as bios or resumes, organizational history, and budget narrative.
Writer	Share document with Copy Editor for input and edits.
Writer	Share all final documents with Records Keeper.

Member	Task
Copy Editor	Cross check with Records Keeper to ensure that all documents and attachments are available.
Copy Editor	Review all documents for consistency of formatting and language. Edit for spelling and grammar.
Copy Editor	Review grant application for clarity and accuracy, grammar, and spelling.
Copy Editor	Review grant application to ensure all questions have been answered, and that information is complete and aligned with grant program goals.
Proposal Coordinator	Schedule and lead committee meetings, set agenda, assign tasks and deadlines.
Proposal Coordinator	Give final approval on grant selection and program priorities.
Proposal Coordinator	Review final grant proposal and give approval for submission. (Determine who will be responsible for submitting final application and all related attachments.)
Proposal Coordinator	Report grants committee activity and active grants to board of directors and other stakeholders. Seek approval as needed.
Proposal Coordinator	Coordinate with business manager to communicate goals and to understand grant's impact on budget.
Proposal Coordinator	Manage committee in accordance with school goals and mission.
Proposal Coordinator	Ensure all committee members are fulfilling obligations and acting with integrity to the grant committee's purpose.

Member	Task
Proposal Coordinator	Provide committee members with training and opportunities for development.
Proposal Coordinator	Consider sustainability of grants committee by continuously recruiting new members and celebrating the work that has been done.

List your committee members and their roles here:

_____

_____

_____

_____

_____

_____

_____

_____

PLAN YOUR PROJECT SCHEDULE

Whether you are working alone or with a team, you need to allow yourself the time it takes to do your best work. Review the list of tasks and any specific requirements for the grant proposal you are preparing, and enter tasks in the chart below to plan your work.

Start with the application deadline, and count backwards from there. Determine how much time you need to gather data and documentation, plan your program goals, develop your budget and timeline, and draft your narrative. Then double it. It always takes longer than you expect.

Name of grant: _____

Deadline for application: _____

Number of weeks to prepare this proposal: _____

Plan your grant-writing schedule.

Week One

☐	
☐	
☐	
☐	
☐	
☐	
☐	
☐	
☐	

Week Two

- [ ]
- [ ]
- [ ]
- [ ]
- [ ]
- [ ]
- [ ]
- [ ]
- [ ]

Week Three

- [ ]
- [ ]
- [ ]
- [ ]
- [ ]
- [ ]
- [ ]
- [ ]

Week Four

- ☐
- ☐
- ☐
- ☐
- ☐
- ☐
- ☐
- ☐

Week Five

- ☐
- ☐
- ☐
- ☐
- ☐
- ☐
- ☐
- ☐
- ☐

SHARE THE NEWS

Once your grants committee is established, it can be helpful to post news about your work on your school's website. Winning grants and sharing your work publicly shows the community and future donors that you are professional and committed to the grants process. It can attract additional donors and support all your fundraising efforts.

As I prepared this document, I was surprised to see the number of schools that don't make donation requests and grants activity visible on their website. If you don't ask, you won't find the support you need.

Use the planning guide below to create your content for a unified fundraising page on your school website. Select and customize the elements that meet your needs.

Possible names for your website page:

- Support (name of school)
- Support Our School
- Support Us
- Give
- Donate

Possible headings or links to sub-pages for more information:

- Volunteering
- Fundraising Events
- Donations
- Foundation
- Grants
- Sponsors/Partnerships

As you create your content for this page, review the section on Transformation to craft a message that celebrates your school's special promise. Describe the features and benefits of your programs, but also share the message of why it is important to support your school.

Grants Page – check each element as you complete it

- ☐ Charge Statement
- ☐ Goals and Priorities for Grants
- ☐ Accomplishments
- ☐ Contact Name and Info

Goals and Priorities

List your grant committee's goals for the current school year and any priorities you have established. Word the statements in parent-friendly language that focuses on the benefits to your community.

_____

_____

_____

_____

Accomplishments

List any major or recent grants your school has been awarded and how those funds contributed to your school's improvement or success.

_____

_____

_____

_____

NO SURPRISES FOR STAKEHOLDERS

Make sure that everyone who will be affected by your grant program is aware of the new project plans. Review each team below and consider how they might need to be involved in helping the project be successful.

Check each item as you complete it. There is also an additional section at the end for you to customize for your needs.

Accounting

☐ Aware of proposed grant and ready for workload

☐ Review plans and provide input

☐ Procedures in place for processing funds according to grant guidelines

☐ Review proposed budget and provide input

☐ Sufficient cash flow available to cover purchases for reimbursement

HR and IT

☐ Aware of proposed grant and ready for workload

☐ Review plans and provide input

☐ Job descriptions and hiring plan in place, if required

☐ HR procedures in place for new employee recruitment and training, if needed

☐ IT procedures in place for new or changing access to technology

Custodian and Facilities Manager

- ☐ Aware of proposed grant and ready for workload

- ☐ Review plans and provide input

- ☐ Plan to provide access to facilities, if needed

- ☐ Plan for custodial support, if needed

Leadership

- ☐ Policies in place that define control, roles, and responsibilities for grant programs

- ☐ Supervision and reporting structure in place for grant project

- ☐ Plan major responsibilities for each grant:

  - Who is responsible for grant-related purchases?
  - Who is responsible for grant-related hiring and training?
  - Who is responsible for grant-related data collection and reporting?
  - Who is supervising the project? What authority does this employee have?

- ☐ Plan for reporting results to board of directors and other stakeholders

Other

- ☐
- ☐
- ☐
- ☐

REFLECTIONS

Reflect on what we've discussed and complete the following statements before moving on to the next chapter.

1.   I learned:

_____

_____

_____

_____

_____

_____

2.   I loved:

_____

_____

_____

_____

_____

_____

3.   I wonder:

_____

_____

_____

_____

_____

_____

_____

4.   I plan to:

_____

_____

_____

_____

_____

_____

_____

Engage

Engage Partners Who Share Your Vision

KEYWORDS AND LINKS FOR SEARCHES

1. Determine the important factors for your school:

    a. Area of focus

    b. Dollar amount needed

    c. Timeline (When do you need the funds? When will program take place?)

2. Begin your search using your favorite Internet search engine, a free grants database, or a paid subscription database.

3. Use **keywords** from the list below to refine your search. Stay focused on these areas for now. If you stumble across a grant that you would like to consider later, simply grab the link and save.

4. Choose up to three grants to review in detail using the Grants Comparison Chart below. Prioritize your list and focus on the grants that best match your current needs.

5. Choose the best match and begin the application process.

Keyword Suggestions

After school program	ELL/ESL/Bilingual	Professional development
Art	Facilities/maintenance	Rural
At risk	Gifted/talented	Special needs
Bullying	Library/media	STEM/STEAM
Character education	Literacy	Technology
Community service	Music	Underserved students

Free Services

*   **FederalRegister.gov** – a daily publication that lists grant information for all federal grants, available by subscription or searchable database

*   **Grants.gov** – an online system for searching current grant opportunities, guidelines, and application packages, used by most federal agencies

- **Catalog of Federal Domestic Assistance** (cfda.gov) – a listing of all grants programs managed by the federal government

- **GetEdFunding.com** – a free listing of most public and private grants for schools

- **Technogrants** – a website that provides links to government technology grants and school grants (www.technogrants.com)

Subscription Database Sites

- EducationGrantsHelp.com

- FoundationCenter.org

- GrantFinder.com

- GrantForward.com

- GrantGopher.com

- GrantSelect.com

- GrantStation.com

- GrantWatch.com

- The Grantsmanship Center (https://www.tgci.com)

- The School Funding Center (https://www.schoolfundingcenter.info/index.aspx)

What is Your Search Strategy?

_____

_____

_____

_____

_____

COMPARE GRANTS AND CHOOSE

Which Grant Is Right for You, Right Now?

Schools are eligible for nearly any grant that accepts applications from nonprofit organizations with 501(c)(3) designations. However, the grants that schools typically most benefit from are construction grants, operational grants, and program grants.

Some grant agencies will accept applications from start-up schools, but many require one to three years of annual financial data as part of the application packet. This can be a problem for new schools that need critical funding support.

Only you can decide which type of grant is right for you, but the biggest factors are:

- What grants are available now?
- What grants are you eligible for?
- What grants support your program idea?
- What grants match your funding needs?

When you are seeking partners to work with you on a grant project, you want to find funders that share your vision and values. This chart will help you compare several grants. Review up to three grants at a time to decide which is the best match for your school.

Grants Comparison Chart

Question	Grant 1	Grant 2	Grant 3
Name of Granting Agency			
Name of Grant			
Is Your School Eligible?			
Funding Max or Range			
Letter of Inquiry or Full Application?			
Deadline			
Notification Date			
Special Requirements			
What are the Donor's Goals and Values?			
What are Your Project Goals?			
Is This a Match?			

Notes

_____

_____

_____

_____

IDENTIFY THE GRANT'S VALUES AND PRIORITIES

In order to meet the funder's goals, take the time to truly understand their goals. Read all available information to learn their core values and priorities. Read the website in detail. Print out the application packet and read it carefully. Highlight any keywords you notice that reflect what's important to them. Then use those words in your proposal to demonstrate your alignment with their goals.

What is the organization's mission and area of focus?

_____

_____

_____

_____

What are the grant's stated objectives or goals?

_____

_____

_____

_____

What keywords do you notice?

_____

_____

_____

_____

_____

What overall theme can you identify?

_____

_____

_____

_____

_____

What do they specifically NOT want?

_____

_____

_____

_____

_____

ASSETS EVALUATION: IMPACT AND CREDIBILITY

Grantmakers want to support innovative programs that offer measurable results (impact) and they want proof that your school is a strong and viable organization (credibility).

Use this worksheet to discover what makes your school a great candidate for the grant partnership you have in mind.

Why is this project important?

_____

_____

_____

_____

_____

_____

What is unique or innovative about this project?

_____

_____

_____

_____

_____

_____

_____

What special skills or experience do your school leaders offer that will make this program successful?

_____

_____

_____

_____

_____

What key relationships have you established with grantmakers, community partners, or other leaders? How can you leverage these relationships to improve your success with this application?

_____

_____

_____

_____

_____

How does this project align with your mission and core values? How does it correlate with the grant's goals and priorities?

_____

_____

_____

_____

_____

What has your school done that will demonstrate your capability to be successful with this project?

_____

_____

_____

_____

_____

What other grants has your school been awarded?

_____

_____

_____

_____

_____

REFLECTIONS

Reflect on what we've discussed and complete the following statements before moving on to the next chapter.

1.   I learned:

_____

_____

_____

_____

_____

_____

2.   I loved:

_____

_____

_____

_____

_____

_____

3.   I wonder:

_____

_____

_____

_____

_____

_____

_____

4.   I plan to:

_____

_____

_____

_____

_____

_____

_____

Execute

Execute Your Plan to Meet Your Goals

4 KEY ELEMENTS

Whether you are talking about a classroom grant for $200 or a federal grant for $20 million, the basic elements of a strong program idea are the same.

- **Vision:** An effective program is based on a strong vision that drives your goals and unites your community.

- **Program:** A program that is innovative and promising is more likely to attract donors and grant funders.

- **Capacity:** Be sure that your school has the resources, experience, and staff to carry out the program and meet goals.

- **Accountability:** You need to know if your plan worked. So do the grantmaker and your leadership team.

In the chart below, check off each statement that is true at this time. Focus on any missing elements and make a plan to resolve any issues.

Vision

- ☐ You have consensus from your administrative team and board of directors to seek this grant.

- ☐ School leaders have a clear understanding of the impact the program would have on your business and school operations.

- ☐ You have buy-in from stakeholders, and you have provided them with a clear understanding of the benefits.

- ☐ You are demonstrating visionary leadership that expresses the WHY of the program in language that inspires others to join the efforts.

Program

- ☐ You have a deep understanding of the problem.

- ☐ You understand what works and what is considered best practice to solve this problem.

- ☐ You understand the target audience for the program and why this program is needed.

- ☐ You have a well-developed rationale for why this solution is most likely to achieve desired results.

Capacity

- ☐ You have a staff structure in place that will support program activities.

- ☐ You have a plan to implement the project with fidelity to the goals and values expressed in the grant proposal.

- ☐ You have planned to allocate or advocate for time and money to develop and oversee the program.

Accountability

- ☐ You understand your goals and objectives, milestones, and responsibilities.

- ☐ You have reviewed any potential roadblocks and have plans to address any anticipated problems.

- ☐ You have a plan to measure progress and make adjustments throughout the program and grant term.

- ☐ You have an evaluation plan to measure and report results to the funder and your community.

DEVELOP A NEEDS STATEMENT

Some grants will ask you to justify why your program or project is needed. This might be done in a few sentences or it may require deeper analysis, depending on the size of the grant and the complexity of the problem you are dealing with. A clear and compelling needs statement can improve your chances of success.

Start with Understanding the Problem

Find the Root Cause

What is a root cause? A root cause is a basic factor that, if removed or corrected, will prevent recurrence of the issue, problem, or behavior under review. You may need to dig deep to find the underlying cause. You don't want to just put a bandage on the surface.

Going back to the purpose statement you wrote for this grant proposal, what is the problem you want to solve?

_____

_____

_____

_____

_____

_____

_____

Ask yourself "why" this is a problem. Then keep asking why until you get to the place where you know you have hit the deeper issue. This strategy is sometimes called "five whys" because it can take up to five levels to get to the root.

For each response to "because," answer with another "why" question and continue until you feel you have reached the root cause.

Why is this a problem? Because...

_____

_____

_____

_____

_____

_____

_____

_____

_____

_____

_____

_____

_____

_____

_____

Collect Data to Inform Your Plans

You'll need to collect and evaluate data to better understand the problem you want to solve. Once you collect this information, you can determine your current status and begin to develop your action plan. You'll compare your current status to your desired status to develop your program goals.

There are three typical sources for this data.

- Survey Results

- Literature Review

- Statistical Data

Survey Results: What do our stakeholders say?

Sometimes you need to get input from the people who are most affected by the problem. Consider if a survey might be informative. Will you ask your students what they think would solve the problem? Will your students' parents be able to provide helpful input? Would your teachers and staff members be able to add value?

You can design a simple survey asking two to five questions that shed light on the problem, and then summarize the results in your grant proposal to support your project plan.

What do your stakeholders say?

_____

_____

_____

_____

_____

_____

Literature Review: What Do the Experts Say?

In many cases, the information you need has already been published somewhere. A quick search on the Internet may reveal articles, books, or websites that you can quote in your proposal. Look for expert opinions that support your plans.

What do the experts say?

_____

_____

_____

_____

_____

_____

Statistical Data: What Does the Data Say?

Consider what data might add to your understanding of the problem. Do you need to review assessment results? Will you look at graduation rates or teacher retention rates? Will you look at enrollment patterns or discipline patterns? What happens when you disaggregate the data into subgroups – does that change the picture or reveal new trends?

What does the data say?

_____

_____

_____

_____

_____

_____

What Is and What Should Be?

A needs analysis answers the question, "What's the difference between what is and what should be?" This can also be called "gap analysis." Ask yourself or your team to consider these questions:

- What is our current status?

- What trends are noticeable?

- What is the expected status?

Your detailed answers to these questions will set the stage for writing the rest of your plan.

Notes

_____

_____

_____

_____

_____

_____

_____

_____

_____

_____

_____

_____

What's the Difference?

Next, we need to analyze the gap between current and desired results. This analysis provides realistic targets for your goals and objectives.

You can use these guiding questions to continue your analysis:

- What is the distance between current versus expected?

- How long do we have to meet goals?

- What do we need to do differently to meet these goals?

_____

_____

_____

_____

_____

_____

_____

_____

Prepare a Needs Statement

The most important point to remember is that a needs statement is never about how much your school needs the money. Your needs statement must describe why your students need the program or the project and how you expect this work to solve the problem you have identified. Ultimately, you are answering this question with your needs statement:

> **What needs to be improved to increase student achievement and how can this grant program support that effort?**

When you write a needs statement, you focus on the problem you want to solve. It takes the reader from "what is the need?" to ""what will you do about it?" You want to demonstrate your understanding of the problem and set up a clear connection between the need you've described and your proposed solution.

For each data source, you will want to provide an explanation of how your proposal addresses that need. Your needs statement should:

- Align with grant announcement and guidelines.

- Communicate your school's experience with the project activities.

- Include concise and compelling anecdotes illustrating the need for the project.

Expand Your Purpose Statement into a Needs Statement

Refer to your purpose statement again. It may provide a starting point for your needs statement. Let's look at a sample purpose statement.

> Many high school students struggle with organization and time management. I want to help by providing a specialized curriculum to teach these skills in Advisory so that they can be successful in school and in their future careers.

In order to create a needs statement, you would support your plans with survey results, data, or expert opinions. Review your notes above and decide what is the most impactful information you want to share.

Example: Imagine that your school has conducted a survey of your secondary students on the topic of organization and time management. You plan to support your proposal with a literature review of current research on the impact of poor time management skills in school. Here is an example of what that might look like:

> A recent survey of the 9th–12th graders at Mountain High School reveals that organization and time management are impacting our students' ability to succeed at school. Eighty-four percent of our students responded "agree" or "strongly agree" to the statement: I struggle to keep track of my homework assignments and due dates. In addition, 79% of students responded "agree" or "strongly agree" to the statement: Late assignments are impacting my grades at school.
>
> According to an article on Learning Works for Kids (https://learningworksforkids.com/2013/11/why-time-management-is-important-to-your-childs-success-at-school/), "Time Management is the

thinking skill that helps children to prioritize tasks and accurately judge the amount of time needed to complete them." The article goes on to state, "From recognizing the need for preparation, to having a good sense of how long assignments might take and being able to prioritize activities, Time Management plays a major role in academic success."

We believe that if more of our students practice effective time management with proven organization strategies, then academic achievement would increase for all our students.

Draft your needs statement here.

_____

_____

_____

_____

_____

_____

_____

_____

_____

_____

_____

_____

_____

DEVELOP GOALS AND OBJECTIVES

Based on your needs statement, what do you want to do to solve the problem? Set your goals and plan your objectives now. Proposals will be evaluated for their fit with the grantmaker's goals. Show how your project clearly advances those goals by reviewing the following criteria.

Develop ambitious but realistic goals.

- ☐ Your goals align with grantmaker's goals as described in the grant application.

- ☐ Keep reviewers and the granting agency in mind by referring to their values and using language that will resonate with the reader.

Offer concrete outcomes.

- ☐ Use numbers to define your expected outcomes.

- ☐ Outputs are measures of program activities, such as the number of students or teachers who participate in the program.

- ☐ Outcomes are changes that result from the program, such as an increase in test scores or college-acceptance rates.

Describe the challenges you face.

- ☐ Discuss why this program needs financial support.

- ☐ Describe any specific hurdles your school is facing that make support from this grant vital to the program's success.

Be realistic.

☐   Develop goals that you can realistically achieve in the given time frame.

☐   Develop goals that have the best chance to solve or reduce the problem.

☐   Develop goals that can be measured with minimum impact on your school staff.

For our purposes, goals are what you want to see as a result of your proposed program or project. Objectives are the specific measurable actions necessary to accomplish each goal. A smaller grant may have only one goal, and two or three objectives. A larger grant will have many more of each.

Review your grant application and related information to be sure you respond to all questions and provide all required information for this important section.

What Are Your Goals?

If you have done the work of developing the needs assessment and needs statement, the goals and outcomes section will practically write itself.

The simplest formula for writing goals is:

From (x) To (y) By (z)

Take the behavior you want to focus on and use your current status as your "from." Then list what you hope the number will be after your grant program has ended and put that number in "to." Set a date for "by." Repeat for as many goals as you need for the project.

An alternative format is:

Increase/Decrease By (x)% By (z)

In this example, you focus on the change you want to see as a percentage of the current status.

Returning to our example of the high school time management curriculum, review the chart below for an example of how you might set up your goals and objectives.

Goal	Objective	Measure
Reduce late assignments by 25% by end of year.	Develop procedures for tracking late assignments across all content areas. Establish baseline percentage of late assignments for beginning of year. Train teachers and students in procedures. Provide effective and consistent support for students with a history of late assignments. Monitor and evaluate results.	Based on beginning and ending number of late assignments as reported in grade books.
Increase academic achievement on end-of-year assessments by an average of 10% over last year's growth rate.	Administer beginning- and end-of-year assessments.	Based on end-of-year assessments for all major content areas compared to beginning-of-year results

Notes

_____

_____

_____

_____

_____

_____

_____

Draft Your Goals and Objectives

Goal	Objective	Measure

GRAB ATTENTION WITH A GREAT TITLE

A creative title provides focus and direction for your proposal. Base it on your purpose statement. Use strong words or unusual combinations to add emotion and excitement.

A great title has three features. The title should:

- **Predict the grant focus**: What subject areas, grade levels, or target population is the grant aimed at?

- **Generate curiosity**: Combine unexpected images or emotional words that will cause the reader to think about what you are saying in a new way or have an emotional reaction.

- **Promise results**: What is the outcome you expect? Help your reader picture the end result that you hope to create.

Ideas for Your Grant Title

_____

_____

_____

_____

_____

_____

_____

_____

BUDGET AND TIMELINE

How Much and How Long Will It Take?

The budget and timeline are critical elements of any grant proposal. This section offers a variety of templates for your use. If your grant application does not provide a specific format for your budget, use what works best for you.

Budget

Template 1

Item	Quantity	Unit Cost	Total Cost

Template 2

Line Item	Total Program Budget	Other Funding	Amount Requested from Grant

Template 3

Category	Expenditures	Revenue from Grant	Other Revenue	Balance

Template 4

INCOME	Amount
Program revenue (ticket sales, admission, tuition, etc.)	
PUBLIC SUPPORT	
Grants (federal, state, or local)	
PRIVATE SUPPORT	
Fundraising	
Grants (private)	
Donations	
Business Sponsorship/Advertising	
TOTAL INCOME	
EXPENSES	
Salaries	
Benefits	
Supplies	
TOTAL EXPENSES	

Timeline

A timeline shows when major tasks will begin and end. It can also include details on who is accountable for each task and how you will measure success.

Template 1

Task	Month	Month	Month	Month	Month

Template 2

You may want to connect activities to goals and objectives	Staff	Year 1				Year 2			
		Q 1	Q 2	Q 3	Q 4	Q 1	Q 2	Q 3	Q 4
Activity/Benchmark	Persons/Agency Responsible	Jan-Mar	Apr-Jun	Jul-Sept	Oct-Dec	Jan-Mar	Apr-Jun	Jul-Sept	Oct-Dec

Template 3

Start Date–End Date	Activity to Achieve Objective	Related Objective and Goal	Evidence that Proves Activity has been Completed OR Data to be Collected from Activity	Persons/Agency Responsible

Template 4

Objective:			
Activities/Strategies to Achieve Objective and Goal	Start Date–End Date	Evaluation Data and Measures (evidence of accomplishment)	Persons Responsible for: A. implementing activity and B. evaluating achievement
1.			
2.			
3.			

PROGRAM EVALUATION

How Will You Know If It Worked?

An effective evaluation plan is built into your action plan. It aligns with your goals and expected outcomes. How will you know if you met your goals? If you created strong goals and outcomes, this will be easy. Keep it simple. Keep it relevant.

Your program will be stronger when you plan effective evaluation measures into the process. Review your goals and objectives. Look at your measures. Create a brief statement that describes how you will define success and how you will measure your results.

As you develop your evaluation plan, you want to be able to answer four questions.

1. To what extent were project activities implemented as planned?
2. How effective was the project in meeting goals and objectives?
3. What was the impact of the project on participants?
4. To what extent were performance targets met?

Create your evaluation plan.

_____

_____

_____

_____

_____

_____

_____

_____

PROJECT SUMMARY

Tell Your Story

In a grant proposal, you are not simply *describing* your project; you are *selling* your idea, your plan, and your potential. You will tell your story in the narrative. This is where you describe your project using descriptive language that demonstrates your excitement and commitment for this work. Evoke emotion in your readers and paint a picture of the better future you see as a result of this project or program.

Review all the basic elements of your grant proposal. Think about any unique purchases you'll be making, how your staff will be involved, and how this project will affect your students. Now, write a summary that describes the most important features of your project in a way that reinforces how important this grant award will be for your community.

Draft your project summary.

_____

_____

_____

_____

_____

_____

_____

_____

_____

_____

_____

REFLECTIONS

Reflect on what we've discussed and complete the following statements before moving on to the next chapter.

1. I learned:

_____

_____

_____

_____

_____

_____

2. I loved:

_____

_____

_____

_____

_____

_____

3. I wonder:

_____

_____

_____

_____

_____

_____

_____

4. I plan to:

_____

_____

_____

_____

_____

_____

_____

Extend

Extend Your Vision with Long-Term Planning

BUILD A GRANTS PIPELINE

A grants pipeline is the intentional approach to grant seeking that develops a steady flow of grant funding for your school.

There are three key components of a successful grants pipeline. You need to support, simplify, and sustain your grant-writing efforts. What does this mean? Take a look at this diagram and think about your school. The grants pipeline concept map shows my vision of a highly effective grants program for schools.

Grants Pipeline Concept Map

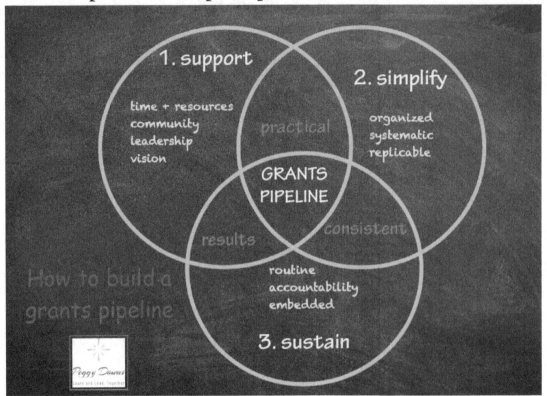

This image highlights the connections between each component, shown at the intersection of the circles. First, you create a system that is practical when you support and simplify your program. Then you are able to be consistent when you simplify and sustain your program. And finally, you produce results when you sustain your program and continue to build support.

The checklist below describes a school with a successful grants pipeline. What's working for you and where can you improve?

1. **Support–All members of the community support the programs funded by the grants and the grant programs align with the school's mission and vision.**

☐ **Time and resources:** You dedicate the time and staff needed to manage the grants process, including searching, writing, and overseeing grants.

☐ **Community:** Parents and staff members understand the importance of grant funding, and cooperate in efforts to manage grant programs.

☐ **Leadership:** Administrators and board members provide consistent leadership and accountability for grants, aligning grant proposals with the school's mission and vision.

☐ **Vision:** Your grant proposals are calibrated to your school's mission and vision, not causing you to veer off in different directions, but rather reinforcing and supporting your core values.

2. **Simplify–Your process to develop and manage grant programs is practical and clearly defined.**

☐ **Organized:** The information a grant writer needs is easy to find and has been edited for consistency and accuracy. You have a tracking system that shows what grants you are interested in, what grants you have applied for, whether you were approved or denied, and deadlines of upcoming grants.

☐ **Systematic:** You have a single person who is accountable for the process, and that person has goals and focus areas to guide grant-seeking efforts. You know your short-term and long-term goals, and these goals align with your school's mission and strategic plan.

☐ **Replicable:** You have the process so well designed that a different person could step in next week and take over the task with no loss of momentum.

3. Sustain–Plans and projects reflect thoughtful attention to long-term goals and consistent focus.

☐ **Routine:** Grants are a regular part of your planning conversations. You or your designated grant writer spend a predictable amount of time managing your grants pipeline (about 5 percent per week, or two hours, once it is established).

☐ **Accountability:** The grant writer reports opportunities, results, and concerns at regularly scheduled meetings. Goals are monitored and reported to the community, and success is celebrated.

☐ **Embedded:** Once established, grants management is simply part of the school culture.

Notes

_____

_____

_____

_____

_____

_____

_____

_____

_____

_____

_____

CLASSROOM GRANTS

Are You Doing Enough?

We've all heard the bad news. It's getting hard to find good teachers. It's getting harder to *keep* good teachers. And when you don't have good teachers who stay with your school, how will you develop good leaders? Who will be ready to step into your shoes when you move on? Think about your teachers as you read the following descriptions.

- **See who speaks up** – Teachers who write classroom grants have a vision. They see a better future for their students and they are able to articulate that vision in a way that resonates with a grant funder. They build support for their idea and they get excited about making it happen.

- **See who steps up** – Teachers who write classroom grants are problem solvers. They see an issue they care about, find a solution, and make a plan. They have the communication and organization skills to develop a proposal and convince a funder to invest in their program idea.

- **See who finishes up** – Teachers who write classroom grants are committed. They have the motivation to follow through on an idea because they believe it will make a difference for their students. They see the project through to the end because it matters to them.

List the teachers that come to mind as you review these descriptions.

_____

_____

_____

_____

_____

_____

_____

Classroom Grants Checklist

Use this checklist to evaluate your readiness for classroom grants.

---

1. Remove any roadblocks to writing classroom grants.

- ☐ Do you have any policies or procedures that inhibit grant writing at your school?

- ☐ Do you provide information and support for grants in a timely manner when asked?

- ☐ Does your response to teachers demonstrate encouragement and support?

---

2. Provide training and resources for classroom grants.

- ☐ Do you provide training in grant writing and implementation?

- ☐ Do you make it easy to get forms and information on reimbursements or purchase orders?

- ☐ Do you provide clear boundaries on what is and is not approved for classroom grants activities and purchases?

---

3. Create a schoolwide culture that encourages teacher initiative.

- ☐ Do you recognize successful classroom grants in your school communications and board updates?

- ☐ Do you provide time and access to information so that teachers can collaborate on grants and other joint projects?

---

4. **Invite teachers who have written classroom grants to join your grant-writing committee or other grant-seeking efforts.**

☐ Do you invite teachers to join your grants committee?

☐ Do you seek feedback from these teachers as you develop new grant proposals?

5. **Develop additional opportunities for leadership development.**

☐ Do you offer increased responsibilities for teachers who are interested and capable?

☐ Do you have an organized process for identifying, testing, and training potential leaders?

☐ Do you have a compensation package established to recognize and reward teachers who take on additional responsibilities?

Teachers stay where they feel their professional needs are being met. Supporting their classroom grant activities not only benefits their classrooms, it benefits your whole school.

Notes

_____

_____

_____

_____

_____

_____

PROGRAM ANALYSIS

Are You Meeting Your Goals?

On a regular basis, you should be able to answer these questions about your grants program, with reports from your committee and by attending periodic meetings.

1. What is the overall effectiveness of our grants programs?
2. How effective is our school's grant proposal writing?
3. How well are we managing the grants we win?
4. Are we making progress toward fundraising goals for approved priorities?

Complete the following chart on a regular basis, with input from your grants committee. This report would be an excellent way to share your grant-seeking results with your board of directors or other stakeholders.

Approved Grants by Quarter

1st Quarter

Grant Name	Purpose	Amount	Approved (yes/no)

2nd Quarter

Grant Name	Purpose	Amount	Approved (yes/no)

3rd Quarter

Grant Name	Purpose	Amount	Approved (yes/no)

4th Quarter

Grant Name	Purpose	Amount	Approved (yes/no)

Notes

_____

_____

_____

_____

_____

_____

GRANTS ADMINISTRATION

Make Sure It All Gets Done

The term grants administration covers all the tasks related to getting a grant and carrying out the project. You can be successful with grants when you ensure your school is meeting the objectives in this checklist.

Grants Administration Checklist

☐   You have instituted ethical practices that align with the school's values.

☐   Your school is in compliance with laws and grant procedures.

☐   You have policies to address operations, responsibilities, and accountability for your grant program.

☐   You have procedures for all grant functions, including financial reporting, transactions, and grant compliance.

☐   You have established a system for finances and program administration.

☐   You have provided adequate training for all employees involved in the grant program.

☐   You have established systems to routinely monitor accountability and evaluation, within a continuous improvement cycle.

Notes

_____

_____

_____

_____

_____

GRANTS MANAGER

Is Your Grants Manager Ready?

Designate one staff member to be your grants manager. It is crucial to have one point of contact for all your grants. Provide training and support to ensure a successful grants program.

Responsibilities

- Coordinate your school's grant-writing efforts
- Track all grants submitted
- Prepare all required grant reports
- Meet all grant deadlines
- Participate in grants committee

Skills and Qualities

- Extremely organized and detail-oriented
- Comfortable working in a spreadsheet or data management system
- Understands how to efficiently dissect a grant application or request for proposals
- Able to answer questions about grants for staff members
- Able to work with your finance department or bookkeeper
- Understands your school goals and grant priorities

Online Grants Training

- FREE courses from Nonprofit Ready (create a free account and search a variety of online courses)
  https://www.nonprofitready.org/grant-writing-classes
- Ed2Go: A to Z Grant Writing
  https://www.ed2go.com/courses/business/operations/ilc/a-to-z-grant-writing

- Ed2Go: Advanced Grant Proposal Writing
  https://www.ed2go.com/courses/business/operations/ilc/advanced-grant-proposal-writing

- Granting Your Vision: Online courses in development
  Check website for updates at www.peggydowns.com/courses

- Grants.gov https://www.grants.gov/learn-grants.html

Grants Certification Program

- https://www.grantcredential.org

Planning

Who will be your grants manager?

_____

_____

How will you train your grants manager?

_____

_____

_____

_____

What additional support will you provide?

_____

_____

_____

_____

_____

WORK WITH A GRANT WRITER

Good grant writers will work with you to ensure your project is cost effective and professional. They can provide expertise, answer questions about your project, and be an important member of your grant-writing team.

Questions to Ask

- How long have you been writing grants?
- What are your primary areas of expertise?
- What is your process for working with clients?
- What are some successes you have had?
- Do you charge hourly or project fee?
- Do you have references from recent clients?
- Are you available for upcoming grant applications?

Recruit a Volunteer Grant Writer

With training and support, anyone can write a grant if they have basic writing skills and an understanding of your school's goals. Consider recruiting a board member or active parent volunteer. Start with small grants and provide support and access to information. You just might find someone who loves it!

Find a Professional Grant Writer

- Contact the author for availability or referrals at peggydowns@gmail.com
- https://www.professionalgrantwriter.org/services
- https://www.grantwriterteam.com

Notes

_____

_____

_____

_____

BUILD YOUR SCHOOL SUPPORT PYRAMID

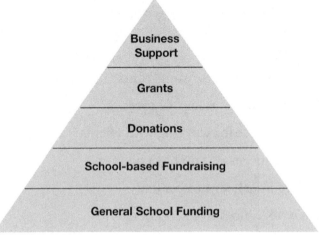

Set Your Goals to Increase Your School's Support Revenue

Use this table to establish your funding plan. Replace the sample data with your own information. You may wish to transfer the information into an Excel or Google Spreadsheet.

Goals

Funding Plan: (Name of School)				
School Year: (2020-2021)				
Most Recent Modification Date: (January 1, 2020)				
	2020-21	**2021-22**		
School-based fundraising	$25,000 25%			
Donations	$15,000 15%			
Grants	$50,000 50%			

Business Support	$10,000 10%				
Overall Goal	**$100,000 100%**				

Tracking

Funding Type	Fundraising	Fundraising	Grant	Business	Donation
Funding Source	Annual Gala & Silent Auction	Fun Run 5K	Daniels Fund	Spectrum Tech	Annual Giving Drive, Donation Program (web & email promo)
Contact Details	nadams@gmail.com	nadams@gmail.com	www.danielsfund.org	dtrace@spectrumtech.com	
Contact Name	Natalia Adams, PTSO President	Natalia Adams, PTSO President	Emily Vance, Exec Director	Daniel Trace, Community Support Liaison	Wendy Hodges, Admin Asst
Amount Requested	$10,000	$5,000	$25,000	$10,000	$5,000
Date Requested or Submitted	Fall 2020	Spring 2020	Spring 2020	Spring 2020	Fall 2021
Assigned To	Wendy	Wendy	Emily	Emily	Wendy
Progress/Results		Scheduled May 6, 2020	Due April 1	Proposal in progress	Planning in progress

SCHOOL FUNDRAISING

I have four important tips that can improve your fundraising efforts.

1. Establish procedures and policies to support your fundraising activities.

2. Keep your fundraising efforts tied to your vision.

3. Set clear and transparent goals, and then share the results with your community.

4. School fundraisers work best when the goals are tangible and familiar to parents.

What fundraising activities have worked best for your school?

_____

_____

_____

_____

What activities will you plan to introduce?

_____

_____

_____

_____

What are your fundraising goals? (How much)

_____

_____

_____

_____

EXTEND

What are you raising funds for? Does this directly affect students?

_____

_____

_____

_____

How will you communicate results with your community?

_____

_____

_____

_____

DONATIONS AND PHILANTHROPY

Donations come from the heart. I have found that these five tips can attract more donations to support your school. Use this page to plan your strategies to increase donations to your school.

Develop Donation Programs

1.   Tell your school's story.

_____

_____

_____

_____

_____

2.   Ask for a specific amount, for a specific goal.

_____

_____

_____

_____

_____

3.   Report on the impact of donations.

_____

_____

_____

_____

_____

4.   Make donating easy.

_____

_____

_____

_____

_____

5.   Say thank you.

_____

_____

_____

_____

_____

Build Relationships with Philanthropists

Philanthropy is a subcategory of donations, where a single patron supports your organization because they deeply connect with your mission.

Who are your potential philanthropists?

_____

_____

Who is the best person to build that relationship?

_____

_____

How will you plan to recognize this long-term investment in your school?

_____

_____

_____

_____

_____

_____

What roadblocks or objections do you see? How can you overcome these?

_____

_____

_____

_____

_____

_____

_____

CORPORATE SPONSORSHIPS

What Is Corporate Sponsorship?

Corporate sponsorship – a donation of money, goods, or services from a corporation or business for a specific event, project, or funding need

5 steps to develop corporate sponsorships

1. Identify potential sponsors

2. Plan your request

3. Make contact

4. Prepare your proposal

5. Follow up

1. Identify potential sponsors

_____

_____

_____

_____

_____

_____

2. Plan your request

_____

_____

_____

_____

_____

3. Make contact

Prepare a script for your phone call or write your inquiry letter.

_____

_____

_____

_____

_____

_____

4. Prepare your proposal

Write your letter formally requesting corporate sponsorship from the businesses you have contacted. Prepare the letter on your school's letterhead using standard business letter format, and have it signed by your school leader if that's not you.

Draft your letter here:

_____

_____

_____

_____

_____

_____

_____

_____

5. Follow up

Make a note in your calendar to contact the organization if you don't get a response in 90 to 120 days (or sooner if required for your request).

_____

_____

_____

_____

_____

_____

BUSINESS PARTNERSHIPS

You can develop more structured partnerships with local businesses. You will be offering access to your families through advertising in exchange for funding.

- **Clearly define your goals** – how much do you hope to attract in new dollars, and what will the new money be used for?

- **Determine your biggest win** – what source of fundraising is likely to provide the biggest impact with the least effort from your staff?

- **Define what you are willing to offer** – will you allow advertising on your website but not on campus? Will you allow advertising on the back of student jerseys for your sports program or would you prefer a gym banner?

- **Clarify responsibilities** – who will track the advertising program and handle any questions or concerns? Who will report results to the board? What data will you share with the advertisers?

Use the following checklist to guide you as you develop these partnerships.

Business Partnership Checklist

- ☐ Do you have policies for advertising, approved by the board of directors?
    - ✓ Pricing structure
    - ✓ Content approval
    - ✓ Vendor approval
    - ✓ Location/duration of ads
- ☐ Do you have advertising information available to interested vendors?
    - ✓ Website
    - ✓ Parent communications (newsletter/emails)
    - ✓ Brochure/one-sheet
    - ✓ Contact information

- [ ] Do you have a plan to encourage greater investment for added value to your advertisers?

- [ ] Do you have a plan for how the advertising revenue will be spent to support your school?

- [ ] Does your accounting department have procedures in place for billing and reporting this revenue?

Notes

_____

_____

_____

_____

_____

_____

_____

_____

_____

_____

_____

_____

_____

REFLECTIONS

Reflect on what we've discussed and complete the following statements before moving on to the next chapter.

1. I learned:

_____

_____

_____

_____

_____

_____

2. I loved:

_____

_____

_____

_____

_____

_____

3. I wonder:

_____

_____

_____

_____

_____

_____

_____

4. I plan to:

_____

_____

_____

_____

_____

_____

_____

Conclusion

MAKE AN AUTHOR HAPPY

A quick favor before you go...would you please leave a review online for this book?

Reviews are very important and help authors like me share our services with others. I am excited get this book into the hands of more school leaders so they can learn to support their schools with grants.

Please take a quick minute to leave a review on Amazon. It helps this book reach more readers just like you. And you'll make an author happy. Thank you!

Leave a review on Amazon

GRANT WRITING FOR IMPACT WORKBOOK

Peggy Downs

DEVELOP A PLAN TO MEET YOUR SCHOOL GOALS

Grants can help schools provide support and opportunities for their students and have greater impact on their communities. I work with school leaders, founders, and teachers to find, develop, and manage grants. To do this, you need resources developed specifically for you.

Through my business and blog, "Granting Your Vision," I provide training, support, and grant-writing services to help you reach your goals. With twenty years' experience in charter schools, I can answer your questions about grants.

What you do is important. Grants can help you do more. My experience in leadership and grant writing helps me understand what you need.

Let's work together to help you do more. You can do this! I can help.

Bonus Offer: Grant-Writing Action Plan ~ 20% Discount

As a reader of this book, you have a special offer waiting for you. I am offering the **Grant Writing Action Plan** at 20 percent off the current price. With my help, you can develop a plan to meet your school goals.

This bonus offer includes a two-hour consultation, a written action plan developed based on your input, and a follow-up call after the plan has been implemented. We'll take my five-step strategy from *Grant Writing for Impact* and apply them to your specific situation, with coaching and resources from me personally.

This offer is limited to availability. Contact me soon to schedule your first call.

Visit www.peggydowns.com/workwithme for more information or contact me for current pricing on this special bonus offer. peggydowns@gmail.com

Granting Your Vision
School Grants Services by Peggy Downs

ABOUT THE AUTHOR

Peggy Downs is on a mission. She wants to help 100 school leaders write successful grants in the next 5 years. In addition to writing grants for charter schools, she provides training and support for school leaders to learn how to write grants and develop grants programs.

Peggy Downs holds a Master's degree in Educational Leadership and a Colorado Principal License. With 20 years experience in charter schools, she has served as a founding parent, teacher, director, and board member. She has supported state and national charter school associations, and has served on the Peer Review Team for Charter School Program (CSP) Grants. She has given presentations at state and national conferences, and was rated a Top 20 Presenter at the National Charter School Conference, #NCSC19.

Peggy Downs writes a weekly blog for school leaders called *Granting Your Vision,* and is the author of the series, **Grant Writing for School Leaders.** She also provides training and consulting services to support school grant programs. Learn more at www.peggydowns.com

Made in the USA
Columbia, SC
25 April 2021